THE **Teen's** GUIDE TO
MODERN MANNERS

THE **Teen's** GUIDE TO MODERN MANNERS

poems

SAM NORMAN

Illustrations by Jack Parham

corsair

CORSAIR

First published in Great Britain in 2016 by Corsair

1 3 5 7 9 10 8 6 4 2

A CIP catalogue record for this book
is available from the British Library.

ISBN: 978-1-4721-5145-2

Printed and bound in Great Britain by Clays Ltd, St Ives plc

Papers used by Corsair are from well-managed forests
and other responsible sources.

Corsair
An imprint of
Little, Brown Book Group
Carmelite House
50 Victoria Embankment
London EC4Y 0DZ

An Hachette UK Company
www.hachette.co.uk

www.littlebrown.co.uk

Contents

SUMMER TERM 79

To my parents and teachers.

Introduction

It all started with Hilaire Belloc. My parents introduced me to his cautionary tales when I was six – probably in an attempt to scare me into behaving myself – and I adored them from the beginning. I loved the thumping iambic tetrameter, the absurdity of the scenarios, Belloc's throwaway rhymes like *foible* and *able*. As time passed, being the irritating little swot that I was, I started trying to imitate them. My protagonist was invariably a boy named Sam, and his list of (literally) fatal flaws was extensive: first he died of neglect after never writing thank you letters, then he froze to death after not wearing a proper coat, and over time he ended up being shot, stabbed, electrocuted and mauled by a bear.

The years went by, and a few months after my seventeenth birthday I was faced with a terrible and seemingly intractable problem. For reasons more foolhardy than wise, I had chosen to take double maths as one of my A levels, and was living to regret it. My teacher had just set us an absolutely laughable piece of work – laughable in the laughing-through-sobs, nihilistic, gallows-humour sense – and I couldn't get a handle on a single question. It was ten o'clock at night. My energy was spent, my morale crumbling. The problems on integration swam before my eyes, mockingly elusive. And then a flash of inspiration struck.

The next day, I swanned into the morning lesson holding a single sheet of paper. Around me, classmates were hanging their heads and weeping over the difficulty of the previous night's work. When my teacher came round to collect our books I held out my offering. He took it, raised an eyebrow and called for silence.

'What's this?'

'It's my homework, sir.'

'Ah. "Young Samuel was a charming child …" A work of fiction, then?'

He proceeded to read it aloud to the class. It was a mock cautionary tale, about a boy named Sam whose maths homework was so traumatically difficult that he went into shock and died. And despite being referred to as fanatical, a psychopath and a vile, sadistic sham, he loved it! It went straight up on his wall and he tried to have it memorialised in the school archives, first through the Maths Department (blocked on the grounds that it wasn't a piece of maths), and then the English (blocked on the grounds that he wasn't an English teacher).

His reaction got me thinking. Everyone was always moaning about the problems with teenagers, so why not dwell on some of these problems in iambic tetrameter? Better still, why not devise gruesome comeuppances specific to these most contemporary of crimes? A teenager writing about teenage flaws – what could be more natural?

For the rest of my time at school, and then over my subsequent gap year, I scribbled away. Siblings, of course, were a rich source of material. After Sam, there followed Mabel (who texted so much that she forgot how to speak), Alice (who refused to go outside without make-up and died in a fire), and a host of others. I grew rather fond of them. Alone in Kathmandu and surrounded by hippies, local delicacies and the pungent fumes of the Nepali bhang, the cautionary tales even prevented me from getting homesick, as they seemed to crystallise part of what it meant to be British.

I had long thought that the poems ought not to stand alone on the page. Belloc's poems were illustrated by B. T. B., and for me, it was those spindly line drawings that really made the verse come alive. Plainly, I too needed an illustrator. Fortunately, when I returned home to get a job, I had someone in mind.

At school, I'd had a friend called Jack Parham – an almost offensively talented person. Head Boy, thespian extraordinaire and a superb linguist, he also nurtured a considerable gift for art. We had both been editors of our school newspaper, and more than once he had illustrated poems of mine for publication (usually as part of last-ditch attempt to fill empty pages). Also – and crucially for my purposes – Jack had the advantage of being a teenager. Soon enough, he was on board and illustrating away with fervour.

Thus it was that *The Teen's Guide to Modern Manners* was born. I wrote the last poem, 'Stanley', a few months after my nineteenth birthday.

This collection is designed to entertain; to pique one's interest and poke fun at a few of the more egregious teenage problems. But for me, it contains another message too. Teenagerdom is seen as a defining time of life. It's also quite a stressful one. On top of the endless academic hurdles, there's an enormous amount of social pressure – pressure to find friends, to have sex, to jump through innumerable hoops to fit in with your peer group. One of the problems of being a teenager is a sense of totality. It's common to think that you'll never find love, never impress your parents, never be successful – and these fears often stem from a sense that your teenage mistakes will shape your entire existence. It is this that *The Teen's Guide* is intended to satirise. In these poems, there are stories of tiny little character flaws that wreck the protagonists' lives; in reality, it's all going to be okay.

WINTER TERM

Chris

WHO TOOK HIMSELF VERY SERIOUSLY AND UNDERWENT A STRANGE REACTION

L——o——n——g, long ago, when Chris was young,
    He was extremely highly-strung.
By nature timorous and shy,
    He'd very freely start to cry
And oh, he'd whine and yowl and yelp
    Until a grown-up came to help!
If caught up in a boyish sprawl,
    He'd let out quite a deafening bawl
And those who heard his frenzied crying
    Would run, believing he was dying.

And yet these tearful, wild polemics
    Were truest with his *academics*.
Young Christopher, it's sad but true,
    Could not stand being number two.
If he came second in a test,
    He'd clutch his hair and grow distressed
And study textbooks all day long
    (And whine they'd marked his script all wrong).
And yet this outlook (oh so grim!)
    Was not entirely down to him.

His parents had, when he was 3,

    Resolved he'd be a prodigy,

So while most kids were learning letters,

    Young Chris was writing operettas,

While other kids had fun outside,

    Young Chris was making aldehyde,

And while they learnt their $\mathbf{ABC}$s,

    Young Chris was reading **WAR AND PEACE**.

His parents were themselves no fools.

Both lawyers, they had certain rules.

They'd whip him up into a fever:

'Young man, you'll be a high-achiever

Or else you're dead to us, you hear?

Now get back to your Edward Lear!

How dare you rest! How dare you fail!

You think that's how you'll get to Yale?

Don't play with other kids! They're rowdy!

You think they'll graduate *cum laude?*

Or just be average. Be our guest.

Feel free to go for second best.

But then, my boy, you won't go far –

At your age, Mozart was a star!'

And so, poor Chris would study Goya

And prep to try and be a lawyer

While both his parents screamed '*try harder!*'

And turned their son into a martyr.

His childhood, as I said above,

Was void of warmth and light and love,

And thanks, regrettably, to this

Were few more highly-strung than Chris...

Alas, this lifestyle, sad to tell,

Will almost never turn out well,

For when a string is stretched too tight,

You know what happens? SNAP That's right.

It happened on some random day

When both his parents were away.
(Since both, of course, were legal giants,
  They had to spend their lives with clients.)
Young Chris was stationed at his desk,
  Defining terms like 'Kafkaesque',
When suddenly, he felt a tingle...
  His senses seemed to meld and mingle,
And then he felt all overcome
  By some great force that left him dumb.
What was this feeling? Very strange.
  He looked around... and what a change!
The songbirds sang! The world had **BRIGHTENED**!
  Chris breathed in deep. He felt enlightened.
His bedroom seemed no longer grey,
  His worries seemed to melt away,
His strain and stress all seemed to cease,
  And, at long last, he felt at peace.

A fortnight on, the court adjourned

And Chris's parents both returned,

And scarcely had they closed the door

When argh! They gasped at what they saw.

Disgusting dishes everywhere.

The sinkhole full of matted hair.

His textbooks lay untouched and dusty.

The house smelled weird and rather musty.

His speechless mother slightly paled,

Before her normal self prevailed:

'Young man! Get down here and explain!'

No answer. Odd. She tried again.

'Come here right now! Don't fool around!'

Still nothing, but a far-off sound…

Now bristling at that son of theirs,

They furiously strode UPSTAIRS

And opened Chris's bedroom door:

'Now… Oh!' She gaped and said no more.

The young lad was indeed inside.

He sat there, dazed and blurry-eyed,
With dreadlocks and some recent stubble,

Quite unaware he was in trouble.
He wore a pendant made of coral,

His scarf was pink, and **very floral,**
His trousers were supremely flared,

From bulky speakers, reggae blared,
And oh, the posters on his wall...

The stuff of nightmares, one and all!
'The world is one', *'I ♥ Nirvana'*,

'There's nothing wrong with marijuana',
'Stand out today. Buy something edgy.'

'No battery farming', 'I'm a veggie!'
'With 9/11 – something odd?'

'Bob Marley = utter god'.

It is a torture like no other
  For any decent tiger mother
To see her one and only son
  Go out and claim 'THE WORLD IS ONE'
And wear a shirt that's trite and trippy
  And be in fact a raging hippie.
She fought for words, and spluttered, 'Chris!
  Just what the hell is all of this?'
He gazed at her, and slowly blinked.
  She looked all blurred and indistinct.
'Whoah there,' he murmured. 'Please don't shout.
  The world's all groovy. **JUST CHILL OUT**.'

His father coughed, and tried to speak –
  Who was this beardy-weirdy *freak*?
'Now stop it, son, I'm warning you—'
  'Hey man, don't tell me what to do.'
They stared. Was this their pride and joy?
  Their darling, straight-A, Yale-bound boy?
Was this their son? This strange intruder?
  This boy who smoked and worshipped Buddha?
And then their darkest worry grew …
  'Hey Chris,' said Dad, 'what's five times two?'
Again, Chris blinked. Whatever next?
  He looked around, a bit perplexed,
And thought about it, scratched his head,

Then peered up, turning slightly **red**.
'Well dude,' he said. 'Not gonna lie …

I'm not a "numbers" kinda guy.'
(His poor old Mum! This made her cry.)

There is a moral to this tale:

Chris never made it into Yale.
And oh, his parents wept and prayed,

And wondered what mistake they'd made.
Just what on earth could they have done

To turn their clever, cherished son
Into a flower-loving yippie,

A raring, pendant-wearing hippie?
The answer's clear: they'd been too pushy!

If they'd been kind and calm and cushy
And let him play outside, quite free,

And even let him watch TV
Their *darling* Chris would not have cracked;

He'd not have *needed* to react!
It's teenage turmoil at its crudest,

That he should go from books to Buddhist.
(Although the East can shed some light

On Chris's miserable plight.
For them, work's good – but so is play.

And as the Buddhists like to say,
It's all about the middle way.)

Lily

Whose pedantic nature turned out to be her ruin

For some, it is a cause of gloom

When people mix up '**who**' and '**whom**'

And get confused with '**lay**' and '**lie**'

And muddle '**me**', '**myself**' and '**I**'.

When this occurs, we shouldn't judge,

But give a gentle, helping nudge

And help them understand the glamour

That comes with having flawless grammar.

If *you* are driven to despair

When using 'there' and 'their' and 'they're'

And think they're frankly all the same,

Don't worry. Don't be racked with shame.

It's fine! We *all* are prone to make

The odd embarrassing mistake,

So when it happens, walk away,

And just remember: life's okay.

However, there exists a type

   Which never fails to take a swipe

Whenever they detect, with glee,

   An incorrect apostrophe.

They'll bawl and bark and cry and clamour

   About the ins and outs of grammar

And how you've got to be precise

   And *never* use a comma splice,

And then, alas, they'll frequently

   Parade your gaffe for **ALL TO SEE**

And slander you and smear your name

   And try to make you weep with shame,

And call you 'stupid' and 'barbarian'

   Because you're not a staunch grammarian.

Now Lily Jones was one of these.

   She found this 'grammar thing' a *breeze*

And always got her spelling right

   And actually was rather bright.

However, woe betide the fool

   Who sat down next to her at school!

15

In English, she would scan your work,

　　Catch sight of something, start to smirk

And then get up and tell the class

　　Your punctuation was a farce!

For her, it was a sort of trauma

　　To see a dodgy Oxford comma.

And oh, a misplaced modifier

　　Would make her *sweat and seethe with ire;*

A run-on sentence, sad to tell,

　　Would warrant CRIES OF ANGST as well,

And how she'd fret and fume and fuss

　　And say that it was *obvious*!

'Oh jeepers! *Surely* you can see?

　　The subject and the verb *agree.*

It's **positive** – you can't use "nor".

　　Right there, you've mixed up "you're" and "your",

And here again, for heaven's sake!

　　It's such a *middle-school* mistake.

Your adverbs are a mess as well,

　　And **wow** – who taught you how to spell?'

The girl herself, grammatically,

 Was just as white as white could be

(Although the language she endorsed

 Could sometimes seem a trifle forced).

There was no **RULE** that she'd not mastered,

 And even if completely plastered

While at some gig, a bleary Lily

 Would turn to you and say (no, really!),

'So – up with whom did Katie hook?'

 (Yes, even then! Right by the book.)

Or else she'd say, and no mistake,

 'Well, out with whom did Danny make?'

The party might be downright wicked,

 She might be absolutely **Liquored**,

But at a show or gig or dance,

 No matter *what* the circumstance,

She felt a crippling inhibition

 At ending on a preposition.

For Lily, this would mean *kaput!*

 No, up with it she **would not** put,

Not now, not once, oh no – not *ever*.

 And though she thought this made her clever,

It was this very mental state

 That brought about her **wretched fate**.

And so, one tragic day, in class,

    The sad occurrence came to pass.

Their homework, all the previous week,

    Had just been to prepare to speak

On something that was close to heart:

    A book; a play; a piece of art.

At Lily's turn – boy, did she preach!

    She gave a stirring, heartfelt speech

On how she found it so romantic

    When boys were pompous and pedantic,

And why, for her, it was erotic

    When they were totally neurotic.

The teacher had begun to doze,

    Till Lily, drawing to a close,

Declared, 'And someone who I know …'

    '*Ahem*,' he coughed. His voice was low.

'With objects, it's not *who* but *whom*.'

    Poor Lily, from across the room,

Abruptly froze, completely smitten.

    She slowly looked at what she'd written,

And there – oh no! – in **BLACK** and white

    Her notes revealed that he was right!

She'd made a **staggering** mistake!

Inside her, something seemed to break.

Not her … How could this be? Oh *why*?

Was everything she knew a lie?

How many ghastly, gruesome slips

Had accidentally passed her lips?

Was she a laughing stock, a **CLOWN**?

Would she get laughed right out of town?

The wretched girl began to stammer,

Attempting to defend her grammar,

But suddenly, her **ABC**s

No longer seemed like such a breeze –

Why *was* it 'whom' instead of 'who'?

Should she write 'to' or 'two' or 'too'?

Which one was plural: 'die' or 'dice'?

When *should* one use a comma splice?

Oh, why was spelling now **SO SCARY**?

How many Cs in 'necessary'?

What was that word she'd never seen?

And *what the hell did 'adverb' mean?*

Well, following this frank exchange

    Poor Lily underwent a change,

And though she didn't know it then,

    She'd **never** be the same again.

Her yearbook entry reads as follows:

    Jus liv ur lyfe wiv LOLs an YOLOs

An booze an buds an cigarettes,

    An jus remember: no ragrets.

From someone who was once so bright

    It's really quite a sorry sight,

And yet, perhaps her sudden **fall**

    Could be a lesson to us all.

It surely shows, I'd put to you,

    That grammar is important, true,

But hey, we make mistakes! We err!

    And life is much importanter.

LILY JONES
YR 9

"Jus liv ur lyfe wiv LOLs an YOLOs an booze an buds an cigarettes, an just remember: no ragrets "

Ben

Whose penchant for computer games led to a sad existence

And now, let's turn to something briefer.
Ben spent hours and hours on **FIFA**,
And all was well, till – oops-a-daisy! –
Ben grew up obese and lazy.

Alice

Whose refusal to venture outside
without large quantities of make-up
proved her undoing

Young girls, we know, are small and nice.

They're made of sugar and of spice

And always, always seek to please

And help out little bumblebees.

They never snap or spit or swear

But try to act with love and care

And seldom play the drama queen …

Well, not till they've become a teen.

At that point, though, they just can't stop

But **binge and booze** and spend and shop

And don't behave as children should

But claim that they're 'misunderstood'.

I don't know if you've ever seen

A raging, tantrum-throwing teen

Who now must face that life is hard

Without her mother's credit card,

And yet I say take heed! **BEWARE!**

They're absolutely everywhere!

For instance, let us look at Alice.

    Her bedroom used to be her palace
Where WICKed WITCHeS met their karma
    Thanks to knights in shining armour.
The girl was charming, blonde and pretty,
    Compassionate, humane and witty,
But though resembling Aphrodite
    She never once was high or mighty,
Subscribing to that age-old law
    That inner beauty matters more.
Respecting all her parents' wishes,
    She made her bed and dried the dishes
And brushed her hair and cleaned her toes
    And never, never picked her nose.
You could not find, in darling Alice,
    The meekest, merest hint of malice.
A nicer child had scarce been seen
    Until – alas! – she turned thirteen.

Her reason, then, became the slave
    Of one great big hormonal **WAVE**,
And though her parents were not rich,
    She'd brood and bark and bite and bitch
Until, at last, she got her way
    (And all too often, sad to say).
If you did not appease her, she
    Would call the NSPCC,
Or beg you, in a shameless manner,
    To buy her **Dolce & Gabbana**,
And starve herself until you caved
    And got the perfume that she craved.
In short, although she sweetly smiled,
    She was a little **MONSTER-CHILD**.

A theatre trip would often be
    The stuff of nightmares, as you'll see.
At six o'clock, her dad would say,
    'Now, Alice, let's be on our way.'
And she'd come back with: 'Just a mo,
    I'll soon be ready, then we'll go.'
And to her bedroom she'd retreat.
    (At this point, you'd put up your feet,
For Alice had it in her power
    To take the best part of an hour.)
You thought she'd never venture out,

And just when you began to doubt
That Alice could be still alive,

She'd loudly yell down, '*Out in five!*'
But '*out in five*', in teenage-speak,

Translates '*perhaps some time next week*'.
You'd **chomp and champ and whine and wail**

And offer cash – to no avail;
Without her lipstick, gloss and rouge,

No threat or bribe would make her budge.

Alas one night it came about

That Mum and Dad were going out
To dine with friends (but not with Alice –

That really was a poisoned **chalice**),
And so the girl was left alone.

She did her nails and checked her phone
And *called her friends* and went online

And scoured the latest Calvin Klein
Then curled her hair and dyed it red

And left the *curler* on her bed.

But in her haste, she clean forgot
That curlers can get very *HOT* …

The **FLAMES AND SMELL** and noise and heat
Drew crowds of people in the street,
When suddenly, a lady cried,
'Oh no! Up there! A child inside!'
Yes, Alice teetered on the edge
Of overhanging window ledge,
Directed there by searing **FIRE**,
Which lapped its way up ever higher;
Then someone kindly dropped a line
And gave the news to **999**,
While someone else set up the call
'Just jump! Come on! We'll break your fall!'
It was quite safe, and not too high,
Yet Alice paused. I'll tell you why …

For teenage girls, a living hell
Is to be seen *au naturel*,
And though a fire should prove a wake-up
That there's a time and place for make-up,
They cling onto their `Golden Rule:`
'*Au naturel*' is never cool.
So Alice had a choice to make:
To jump or else be turned to **steak**.

There rang out crashes, cracks and cries …

Dystopias flashed before her eyes,

And wrenched apart by such a choice,

She shouted in a fearful voice,

'My hair's not done! I look a mess!

The 60s called – they want their dress!

I hate this top! Who bought these shoes?

I can't be seen – I just refuse!

Why live, if it means social death?'

So spoke she with her final breath,

And pondering such public shames,

She made her choice, and **CHOSE THE FLAMES**.

Zak

Who always left his clothes on the floor until they eventually swallowed him up

Zak left his laundry on the floor.

It piled up **more** and **more** and **more**

Till Zak got lost and died, one day,

Which shows you: **put your clothes away**!

Chloe

Whose fashion-sensitivity almost got her killed

I wonder if you've ever sensed

How fervently girls fight against

This maddening parental wheeze

To 'wear some proper clothes, hon, *please*'.

Such sound advice is seldom wise:

It prompts a volley of replies

Like 'Mum, for heaven's sake, don't sweat it,'

'It's fashion, Dad, you wouldn't get it,'

'Oh *Mum*, parental views are banned,'

'Pur-*lease*, you just don't *understand*!'

This teenage angst is running rife –

This '*You know nothing; it's MY life*' –

And no one better shows this trend

Than Chloe Smith, my cousin's friend,

Whose penchants almost proved her end.

Young Chloe, from her earliest youth,
Was something of a **fashion sleuth**,
Who found it child's play to gauge
What was or would be all the rage.
If you had bought some brand-new shoes
And asked young Chloe for her views,
She'd smile politely, out of pity,
And say, 'Oh yes, they're almost pretty,
But *purple*, honey, with your skin?
Plus, slip-ons aren't exactly 'in'.
Your handbag, though – that's *nearly* chic,
So what that spots are *so* last week?
Your hair looks really gorgeous plaited,
But *eugh*, that bow – and while we're at it …'
And then she would **soliloquise**

On how your dress clashed with your eyes
And why your earrings didn't work
And how your socks would make boys smirk
And why your top was out of style,
But *hey*, you had a lovely smile!

Yet though she thought herself an artist,

　　Her clothing choices weren't the smartest

For Chloe had a special law –

　　To put it briefly: **less is more.**

The fewer clothes she wore, the better.

　　Who even needs a scarf or sweater?

It might be cold. It might be snowy.

　　Yet nonetheless our hero Chloe

Would often try to leave the house

　　In nothing but a skimpy blouse.

Her parents – poor, well-meaning fools –

　　Endeavoured to lay down some rules.

'You can't go out like that. **IT'S FREEZING.**'

　　'Oh sweetie, look at you – you're sneezing!'

But did she crumble? Not a bit!

　　In fact, she rather relished it.

'Just *try* to make me wear that fleece –

　　I *swear* I'll call the fashion police!

Oh yes, that jacket's really nifty;

　　　　It's not remotely **1950**.

　　A coat? Oh, what great thinking – NOT!

　　　　Who am I? **Robert Falcon Scott**?'

And then, although they said she'd freeze

　　　　(It being minus two degrees),

Their prayers and pleas and hopes and tears
　　Would fall, alas, on stone-deaf ears,
As Chloe had a short refrain:
　　That looking nice involves some PAIN.

Well, at this juncture in our story
　　The poem almost gets quite gory,
So readers with a nervous heart
　　May well prefer to skip this part.
Let's set the scene. Her term had ended.
　　What's more, the school that Chlo attended
Had organised a **science** outing
　　To Greenland, for some puffin-scouting.
Now Chloe was of course no naysayer –
　　She'd love a selfie with a glacier! –
And so she swiftly packed her bags
　　And gathered all her fashion mags
And did her hair and read a book
　　And checked the drinking age in Nuuk
And softly hummed her favourite song –
　　Now what could **possibly go wrong**?
A trip with friends? A week away?
　　Oh yes – the *perfect* holiday …

Well let's just say that four days on,
    This sunny attitude was gone,
For Chlo by now was feeling silly
    And, truth be told, a little chilly.
Her friends had, sensibly enough,
    Packed coats and scarves and other stuff,
And mainly done as they'd been told
    To wrap up warm against the **COLD**,
While *Chloe*, on the other hand …

    Well, it was colder than she'd planned.
In fact, she felt, it was obscene:
    This land was not remotely green!
Could she be blamed? How could she know
    That there'd be wind and ice and snow?
The simple truth was poor old Chloe
    Had packed attire less warm than showy,
Like tights and heels and skimpy shirts
    And itsy-bitsy miniskirts.

38

But boots and gloves? A woollen scarf?

Oh goodness, no – don't make her laugh!

She **loathed** these garments with a passion.

They were *supremely* out of fashion.

So when the helpful local guide

Proposed she wear his coat outside

A steely glow came to her eyes.

Oh no! There'd be no compromise!

His coat was foul. She wouldn't wear it.

She'd simply have to grin and bear it.

The more and more the guide insisted

The more she violently resisted

And shook her head and caused a din

Until he finally gave in,

But even then she **shook** with verve.

That *he* should lecture *her*! The nerve!

Who was this man? A dunce! A dimwit!

That silly, irritating Inuit!

He had no right to choose her clothes!

Who were these pesky **Eskimos**?

Her friends might be more aptly dressed,

But hey, at least she looked the best.

Yet sure enough, her every friend
    By now was almost at wits' end,
All thanks to Chloe's endless **groaning**,
    Her baseless (vaguely racist) moaning:
'My body isn't made for hiking –
    Unlike our guide, I'm not a Viking!
Two minutes! That's what we were told.

Hey guys, wait up! I'm really cold!'
And yet, despite this constant whining,
    There was, at least, a silver lining:
Without a sweater, gloves or jacket,
    Poor Chloe simply couldn't hack it!
In spite of how she whined and whined
    The girl got cold and lagged behind
(To which the guide stayed strangely blind),
    And soon young Chlo was just a speck.
But did they worry? Did they heck.

And yet, in fact, the girl reflected
  She had no grounds to feel dejected –
This was no sudden, dreadful crisis.
  Her art demanded sacrifices!
What's more, despite her vast self-pity,
  She'd soon be **warm** and in the city –
Or so she thought, misguided child:
  In Greenland, polar bears roam wild …

To all the little girls out there:
  Try not to meet a **polar bear**.
Though some are gentle when you're near,
  It's usually a bad idea
As mostly they're a surly bunch
  Who view you, principally, as *LUNCH*.
The one with Chloe in its gaze
  Had eaten not a thing for days
And as it stood, erect with poise,
  Its **stomach** made a funny noise.
Oh ho, it pondered. *Lucky me.*
  She's more than satisfactory.
And, rather pleased with its selection,
  It trotted in the girl's direction,
Perceiving with a happy nose
  A gratifying lack of clothes.

Well Chloe, having taken stock,

    Received a rather nasty shock,

For it was not quite every day

    MAN-EATING MONSTERS came her way.

The normal food chain, she opined,

    Was really rather well designed

And, used to being at the top,

    She wasn't keen for this to stop.

The poor girl squeaked. She was a goner!

    The bear was basically upon her!

(*Oh my*, it thought, *she looks delicious.*

    Full-bodied, wholesome, and nutritious.)

What could she do? What hope was there

    Against a great big polar bear?

Oh why had she so loved to party?

    Why couldn't she have learnt *karate*?

The massive beast came ever closer
Towards its soon-to-be samosa,
 Till she could see its deadly **claws**
Its foaming, frothing, fearsome jaws,
 Its giant bulk, its gleaming eyes –
('*Yoo-hoo!*' they seemed to say. '*SURPRISE!*')

The poor girl teetered on the spot.
 Well, this was it: her only shot!
Her chance to stave off death, or worse.
 She plunged her hand inside her purse
And grabbed some perfume, whipped it out,
 And threw it at the creature's snout.
It whistled in a lovely arc
 Then – *oof!* – it crashed into its mark!
The great bear stopped, no thought for slaughter.
 It blinked. Its eyes began to water.
That really had made quite a smack.
 Its prey had never once fought back!
Why *was* that girl so cruel and curt?
 Those perfume bottles really hurt!

And as it rocked there, DAZED, unsure,

    It wondered: would the girl have more?

She might well have enough cologne

    To make this place a combat zone.

That *would* be bad. Oh no! Code Red!

    And so it panicked, **turned and fled**.

Well, after this amazing bout,

    I'm glad to say it all worked out,

And though it might sound rather strange,

    Young Chlo experienced a change.

She soon caught up with all her friends,

    Apologised and made amends,

And gave the poor guide quite a scare

    With stories of the **polar bear**

(And oh, the bear – let's not forget:

    It ran off, hungry and upset,

But please don't fuss: it had its meal –

    A rather juicy baby seal).

And now, there's just one thing to say:

    If you should meet young Chlo today

Upon a freezing winter's night,

    She'll likely cut a funny sight,

Wrapped warm in coat and scarf and snood

    And **woolly** socks, if in the mood,

Because she knows what matters most

    Is that she'll be as warm as toast.

She needs no heels or skirts or make-up.

    Her Arctic exploits proved a wake-up!

And fashion? Well, she's pretty sure

    It's not worth being **frozen** for.

SPRING TERM

———

Pete

Who fell victim to his poor people skills

Now Pete was at that awkward stage,
    That clumsy, adolescent age
When first you feel the strange effects
    Exuded by the gentler sex.
So Pete, disliking life alone
    And driven by testosterone,
Bought chocolates, flowers, strings of pearls,
    To try and woo the lucky girls,
And read John Donne and lost some weight
    And did his best to stand up straight.
(And all to try and get a date!)

For us, of course, it's very easy
    To think that Pete was all too sleazy,
And yet, this wasn't really so.
    Perhaps he was a trifle slow,
And struggled to remember faces
    And had some **hair** in nasty places,
But really, Pete was rather nice.
    He kept his head down, took advice,
Was always courteous and polite
    And didn't have an ounce of spite.
He was that rarest thing to find:
    A boy who was sincere and kind.

And so it should be no surprise

That Pete stood out from other guys,

And soon enough had found a date:

A charming, *pretty girl* called Kate.

(Who says true love can't find its mate?)

At once, the birds began to sing,

For Kate was Peter's everything!

He treasured and respected her,

He never once neglected her,

But they'd hold hands for **days and days**,

Existing in their special haze

(And having shameless PDAs).

A better match, you never saw.

    But oh! Pete had a **fatal flaw.**

I said he was a little slow,

    And yes, poor Kate's dim-witted beau

Did something that would make her huff:

    He didn't really notice stuff!

Oh how it made her **stomp and swear**

    Whenever she had done her hair

And walked right past him, showing off,

    And gave a little hinting cough:

'Hey Petey, honey, whatcha think?'

    He'd look up, turn a little pink,

And then – the poor, benighted clot! –

    'What do I think? About, er, what?'

What folly! What an aberration!

    To girls, a second's hesitation,

A moment's pause, an instant's 'er',

    Is out-and-out anathema.

Alas, he couldn't get it right.

    Poor Peter cut a sorry sight

When Kate, with a foreboding ring,

    Said, *'So, you notice anything?'*

Oh how he floundered, flapped and flailed!

    He'd have a guess, but always failed!

A sad occurrence, you'll agree –

A dreadful, real-life tragedy,

 For boys did not come any sweeter

Than dearest, darling, dorky Peter

 Who always, always tried his best

To analyse how Kate was dressed

 And whether she had done her nails

Or got a handbag at the sales,

 But oh, the boy was simply useless.

He couldn't do it. **No excuses.**

One day Kate made herself a bet.

 She was, by nature, a brunette,

But how (she thought) would Pete respond

 If she should dye her hair bright blonde?

Quite soon, the process was complete.

 Now blonde, she went to visit Pete

Who **hugged her**, hazily aware

 Of something strange about her hair,

And then, they just hung out (with Kate

 Becoming more and more irate)

Until after an hour, or three,

 She flatly asked, 'Pete. Whatcha see?'

(The poor boy quailed. What could it be?)

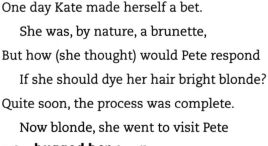

'You, er … Your ears?' he tensely said.

Kate frowned, and **slowly shook her head.**

Poor Peter quaked. 'Well, um … Your lipstick?'

She scowled, and thought *You stupid dipstick.*

He racked his brains. His final guess.

Her feet? Her front? Her face? *Oh yes!*

It was quite small – could he be blamed?

But in a loud voice, Pete proclaimed

(Unwittingly supremely harsh),

'*I know! You've shaved off your moustache!*'

We shouldn't be too cruel, because

He simply said it as it was.

He never cared for masquerade

And always called a **spade a spade**,

And to be fair, this brusque review

Was actually entirely true.

However, what our young friend lacked

Was just a modicum of tact,

And there's a lesson here to take,

So you don't make the same mistake.

No matter when, what, how or where,

Don't ever diss a lady's hair!

DON'T DO IT. No. I promise you.

It won't end well, for if you do

Kaput! It's over! Deal-breaker!

You're toast – prepare to meet your Maker.

As Peter spoke, he felt a chill.

Kate stared at him. If looks could kill …

And then he twigged. Oh gosh! Repent!

'Er, Katie darling, what I meant …'

Her glower made his voice diminish.

She didn't even let him finish,

But left poor Pete to cringe and wince.

And he's been single ever since.

Jenny

Who learnt the hard way the importance of being precise

And now, a word on being clear.

    With Jenny's *birthday* getting near

Her parents asked her what she'd like –

    A dress? A purse? A brand-new bike?

But Jenny gave them not a clue:

    'Oh Mummy, *anything* from you!'

Alas, the silly, senseless klutz!

    They gave her socks, and Jen went **NUTS**.

Stanley

Who let his facial hair get out of control and suffered for it

There was a youth called Stanley Wilde –
    A rather irritating child.
Quick-witted, handsome, great at sport,
    Well liked by all – you know the sort!
He was, at once, extremely cool
    And maddeningly good in school,
At which he won all sorts of prizes –
    Both big and small, all shapes and sizes –
Yet always put it down to fluke.
    Does it not make you want to puke?
What's more, this boy whom all revered
    Was not at all inept or weird.
His social life passed in a whirl!
    He seldom was without a girl,
But seemed to know how long to stay
    Or where to go or what to say
And always had the perfect shirt
    And knew exactly how to flirt.
Young Stanley was – and let's be straight –
    The kind of guy we love to hate;

What with his friends and girls and looks
    And artiness and love of books
And massive scholarly success
    And general **chiselled manliness**
It all just seems too much to swallow!
    Well, worry not. There's more to follow ...

As you'll have gleaned by now, young Stanley
    Took lots of pride in being manly,
And was at quite advanced a stage
    Compared to other kids his age.
This mostly meant that he was tall
    And came out better in a brawl,
But one day, Stanley grew aware
    That he could boast some facial hair.

(This hair was nothing great, for sure –

A light lip-sprinkling, nothing more –

Yet as it SPROUTED, bit by bit,

He grew immensely proud of it.)

His friends were not the biggest fans

Of this new attribute of Stan's

And oh, his parents made a fuss

And thought it rather hideous.

They tried to nag and plead and scoff

('For heaven's sake, just shave it off!')

But there it stayed, for public viewing.

He loved it dearly. **Nothing doing.**

The school was soon in quite a twist.

They couldn't technically insist

And force young Stanley into shaving –

He wasn't really misbehaving,

And can you really be so tough

On thirteen-year-old facial fluff?

The dangers were, in fact, **immense**.

It might impair his confidence

And start a long parental feud

And end up with them getting sued.

Good gosh, no! They could all agree
    By far the safest policy
Was just to let the infant be.

Quite soon, young Stanley's **PEACH-LIKE** fuzz
    Was causing an enormous buzz,
For he by now had quite a headful –
    Which, truth be told, looked really dreadful.
The worst part was a furry strip
    Which sat above his upper lip
Like lightish, whitish, wispy wool,
    And made him quite unkissable!
His social life was looking grim.
    No girl would now be seen with him.
Where once his Friday nights had been
    Him tearing up the party scene,
He now would lounge on his settee
    With pizza and Love Actually
Not realising, sad to say,
    His life was just a shave away,
But feeling rather down and glum.
    Alas! Much worse was yet to come …

Dear governors,
I cordially invite
myself to your
school.
Yours royally,
H. R. H xxx

A fortnight on, behind closed doors,

    The seventeen school governors

Were locked in quite a panicked chatter

    About a rather urgent matter.

Though absolutely unexpected,

    The school had somehow been selected

To break from everyday routine

    And host *Her Majesty The Queen*!

Well, patently, I'm sure you see

    Just how traumatic this must be,

For it can stress you something chronic

    To have to entertain a monarch,

Especially when the chosen day

    Is only just a week away.

Quite overwhelmed by everything,

    At that point they were **labouring**,

As though they just had hours to live,

    To find a representative –

An envoy from among the students,

    A child with taste and poise and prudence

Who'd show around the royal guest
    And leave her happy and impressed,
And show the college at its best.

So there they **argued** and discussed:
    Which student could they really trust?

'There's Alex Brown,' the chairman said,
    'But mentally, the boy's quite dead.
Of course, there's Wendy Jones as well,
    But, to be frank, she's dull as hell.
Bob Mitchell's always sniffing glue,
    And Mary Clarke would never do.
Grace Yusuf's known for telling porkies,
    Fred Black is terrified of corgis,
Dwayne Howard is a stupid child –
    But what about that Stanley Wilde?'

This seemed to him a good suggestion.

    The boy was smart enough, no question,

And charming, yes, with perfect grades,

    And cool self-confidence in spades –

But straight away his words were met

    With general **murmurs of upset**,

And soon it had become quite clear

    It was a horrible idea.

'I don't suppose, Your Chairmanship,

    You've ever seen his upper lip?'

'Oh yes, the boy's got charm to spare,

    But oh my gosh, his facial hair …'

'You know, that stuff can really grate ya.'

    'He's Wilde by name and wild by nature!'

'His fuzz can leave you feeling bruised.'

    'I doubt Her Maj would be amused …'

The chairman, having got the gist,

    Reluctantly did not resist,

~~But struck young Stanley off the list.~~

To cut a longish story short,

   They found a boy called Benny Court,

Whose love of dogs entranced the *Queen*

   (Despite his dozy, dopey mien).

In fact, she'd so much time for Ben,

   That she appointed him, right then,

Her *Private Royal Pooch Vizier*

   (A post of sixty grand a year!),

And there he prospers, thanks to this,

   Content in comfy, canine bliss.

Young Stanley, on the other hand …

   Well, life did not turn out so grand.

His hair grew out. His grades went down.

   He'd soon become the schoolroom clown,

And if you saw his class today,

   You'd doubtless spot him straight away:

Sat at the back, he lolls around;

   He never speaks, or makes a sound,

But lounges there, a hopeless slacker

   (Who looks a little like Chewbacca).

Serena

Whose habit of fishing for compliments
led to a miserable life

It's really an enormous pity
    When young girls who are rather pretty
Take modesty just way too far
    So people say how great they are.
The clearest case of this demeanour?
    My little sister's friend Serena,
Whose harrowing decline and **f**a**ll**
    Should be a lesson to us all.
The girl was pretty, blonde, petite,
    Quite popular and rather sweet,
And yet she had a fatal fix.
    Serena always got her kicks
From people saying she was fair
    And how she must have friends to spare
And how they really liked her hair.

The girl would go out on a limb
    To be told she was oh-so-slim
And *how* would she accomplish that?
    By claiming she was 'feeling fat'!
At this her siblings, friends and mother
    Would clamber over one another
To set the record nice and straight
    And tell Serena she was **great**.
(No wonder she'd self-deprecate!)

It was unique. You should have seen her.
    If you were walking with Serena
And said that someone else looked nice,
    Poor fool! You'd have to pay the price.
That phrase would make the gloves come off.
    'But I look rubbish.' *cough cough cough*
And then Serena would not rest
    Until you said you liked her best
And hailed her looks, her taste, her leanness,
    And said that she resembled *Venus*.

It drove her classmates round the bend,
　　This plaudit-fishing without end,
But what to do? They knew that she
　　Would kill them if they dared *agree* ...
So when she voiced her cares out loud
　　A swarming, fawning, gushing crowd
Would swoop on in to tell her 'No!
　　Serena! How we love you so.
How dare you say you've put on weight
　　When, *Jeez Louise*, you're looking great!
You can't believe you look a mess.
　　The Ancient Greeks fought wars for less!
Oh baby, if you only knew –
　　We'd kill if we could look like you.'

Yet as this happened more and more,

    This mindset that we all abhor

Became entrenched inside her psyche.

    Good gosh! I hear you cry. *Oh crikey!*

And yes, she couldn't help but do it.

    It was so easy: nothing to it!

However, in the world today

    This kind of fishing doesn't pay,

And often, though some loathe and lump it,

    It really helps to **blow your trumpet**.

No decent university

    Would even sniff at her CV,

For as it happened, sad to tell,

    She didn't sell herself too well.

Achievements? *None, I'm really bad.*

    Or inspirations? *Just my dad.*

Ambitions? *Um, I'd like to grow.*

    Well, passions? Interests? Hobbies? *No.*

Your academics? *None too smart.*

    So, weaknesses? *Oh, where to start!*

Now everyone around her knew

    That none of this was really true.

Serena was astute and bright;

    Her academics were all right.

If she'd just told the truth, then she'd

    Have strolled right on in, guaranteed,

But no! Expecting contradiction,

    The girl had handed in pure fiction

(And all to sate her strange addiction).

    So now ... Oh, where should I begin?

At once, the letters flooded in:

    'We're sorry, we just can't accept you.'

'The field was strong – we must reject you.'

    'Your record's not quite there, we fear.

'It's "no" from us, but try next year!'

    In short, their answers were alike:

They told the girl to take a hike.

So thus distressed, depressed and anguished,

    A weaker girl might just have **languished** –

Not so for her! Without a sigh,

    She got back up, her head held high,

And looked for work she thought might suit her.

    A nurse? A vet? A music tutor?

A stewardess? A shop assistant?

    No luck, but still she was persistent,

And then, after a month or two,
   Serena got an interview!
At once, she felt enthusiastic.
   The job was good, the pay fantastic.
All she had to do was preen
   And model in some magazine.
(The perfect job for any teen.)
   Of course, there was the interview,
Which could be rather hard – but **pooh!**
   It must be a formality:
How tricky could it really be?

And so, the fated day soon came.
   She went. A man read out her name,
And then without much more ado:
   'Hello, young lady, how are you?'
The interviewers seemed quite nice;
   She did her catwalk once or twice,
And then she postured, preened and posed,
   And all was dandy, she supposed.
In time, a lady said, 'Thanks, hon.
   A few quick questions, then we're done.
We want a girl with **dreams** and **drive**,
   A girl who clearly feels alive
And likes the way she looks, as well.

So tell us: why d'you think you'd sell?'
Serena smiled. At once she knew
    Exactly what she had to do.
(And if you find this slightly strange,
    Remember this: she *couldn't change*!)

'I doubt,' she proudly said, 'I would …
    I don't think I'd be any good.'
The lady frowned, one eyebrow raised,
    'Perhaps it's better I rephrased:
Just leave your manners on the shelf
    And tell us why you like yourself.'
The girl half-chuckled, in the zone.
    For faux self-doubt, she stood alone.
'I don't at all!' she said with glee.

    No luck. She coughed suggestively.
'All right,' the lady said. 'That's fair.
    But surely, love, you like your hair?'
'Oh that's the worst part,' trilled the girl.

'It never dries and just won't CURL.

Oh no, I utterly abhor it –

Imagine if your readers saw it!

They'd likely vomit there and then!

They'd never buy your stuff again!

Oh Jeez, it gets all limp and floppy:

You wouldn't sell a single copy.'

The lady stared. Serena smirked.

She'd **nailed** her act. It must have worked.

The girl leant back and closed her eyes,

Awaiting their protesting cries –

Alas, poor child, she was unwise,

For no one moved to contradict her.

What was this? Had her senses tricked her?

No sound. No movement. Not a word.

Perhaps they hadn't really heard.

Serena counted up to ten.

'My hair …' she laboured once again,

And gave another hinting cough.

They told her gently: **bugger off**.

Well now there's little else to say,

   Except what you should take away

From poor Serena's tragic case

   Is that you can be fair of face

And popular and quite a flirt

   And own the latest miniskirt

And have outrageous hair and flaunt it

   And get whatever else you wanted,

But there's one thing we all would wish:

   You've got it. Great. *Now please don't fish!*

SUMMER TERM

James

Whose flagrant disregard for personal
hygiene changed his life for the worse

From Marrakech to Timbuktu,

   From Vietnam to South Peru,

From Loch Ness and the Scottish Highlands

   Way down to the Aeolian Islands,

From SCORCHING HEAT to sleet and SNOW,

   In fact, no matter *where* you go

There's something that you'll doubtless find

   Is always true of humankind.

What is it? Some inherent vice?

   That everybody has their price?

That there's no point to all our labour?

   That no one *really* loves their neighbour?

Oh no, it's simpler (sad to tell):

   It's just that boys will always smell!

It's widely known that being clean
    Proves just too much for any teen,
For even in the time of Moses
    Poor parents had to hold their noses
And whine and wail and plead and hope
    That someday kids might take to soap.
And yet one boy, I would suggest,
    Stands proud and tall above the rest:
Great scholars deem this kid to be
    The **smelliest** in history,
And claim, when all is said and done,
    He's easily the number one.
So what's his name? I hear you cry.
    This shower-shunner – who's the guy?
Now look. You should be well aware
    That gossiping is most unfair.
We shouldn't give this poor kid **FLAK**,
    Especially behind his back,
And as a rule, I don't name names,
    But oh my gosh – if you'd met James …

He wasn't always so. It's true.

He ran around as children do

And **climbed up trees** and got in fights

And muddied up his cricket whites.

Up to the age of twelve did James

Indulge in japes and childish games,

And though he went round raising hell,

At no point did our young friend *smell*.

But then there happened something strange,

For all this was about to change –

And, oh! The day he turned thirteen

His whiff would make you go bright green!

From that point on, James knew no bounds.

He never showered, on the grounds

That soon he'd **sweat** some more, and then

He'd have to shower once again.

His **pong** brought tears to the eyes

Of those below a certain size

And goodness, those who smelt his breath

Got on their knees and prayed for death.

His pungent, overpowering whiff

Was so intense that just one sniff

Made babies bawl and adults start –

And did I say *HE LIKED TO FART*?

Whenever James got back from school
　　He'd dump his bag down, as a rule,
And then he'd **lounge** before the telly,
　　Devouring food from next door's deli
(And getting really very smelly).
　　With motivation running low,
He'd STEW there in his own BO
　　And curl up – sticky, stuffy, sweaty –
With wrappers strewn round like confetti
　　Before – oh Lord – before he'd choose
To take off his DISGUSTING shoes
　　And stink out the entire street
With his revolting, rancid feet.

The lifestyle of their son and heir
Drove James's parents to despair,
And though they did all in their power
To get their boy to take a shower
Still James would simply not comply.
Confused? Well let me tell you why.

It's something everyone should know:
You can't detect your own BO!
And so although his dreadful smell
Made Mummy's life a living hell,
And though the stuff between his toes
Wrought utter **havoc** on the nose,
And though his underarms were cheesy,
And though his breath would make you QUEASY,
He wouldn't change, the little brat.
He saw no problem. That was that.

Let's pause a moment, if we may.
When planning out your holiday
There's nothing quite so middle-class
As choosing to get off your arse
And leave behind life's rough and tumble
To go exploring in the jungle.
Accountants, lawyers – they all do it:
Pack their bags and holler 'SCREW IT!'

It's one of their most basic drives,

    To brighten up their dreary lives

And throw in just a splash of colour

    To work that couldn't be much duller.

They simply love the **Kalahari**

    And rhino-spotting on safari

Where they'll ensure that, just for laughs,

    They get some selfies with giraffes.

Now James's dad had this conundrum

    (Just how to make their lives less humdrum)

And summer was already near,

    When … What was that? **A GREAT IDEA**!

He called the family straight away:

    'Guys – soon we're off on holiday

And I know just the spot. It's corking!

    You all can call me Stephen Hawking.

We'll buy our tickets and MEANDER

    All the way to South Rwanda,

Then hire a guide and – here's the killer –

    Try and search out a gorilla!'

They loved it! James's mum could boast
    To all her friends while playing host;
His sister, little baby Nell,
    Would have something for show-and-tell;
And James, whose feet by now were fungal,
    Could get some pictures *#jungle*.
It all was perfect. Soon enough
    They'd packed their bags and they were off.

A fortnight later, be it said,
    Their confidence had turned to dread,
Though at first glance you wouldn't think
    That anything was out of sync.
The guide spoke English. Food was nice.
    They'd got it at a decent price.
They'd come in prime **gorilla** season –
    Surely, then, they had no reason
For all these doubts, these second thoughts?
    Well, three words: *James's boxer shorts*.

Long days of trekking, sad to tell,

    Had not done much for James's smell,

And in the sticky, *sultry heat*,

    His armpits – eugh! And oh, his feet!

He sweated like a pig, and – gosh –

    There was no way for him to wash!

His sister had begun to whine,

    The guide had threatened to resign,

And as the hours rolled on by

    They wanted to curl up and die.

Then, just as they were on their knees,

    They reached a clearing in the trees.

The guide stopped dead. Without a word

    He gestured forwards. Something stirred.

They didn't dare to move a muscle

    When, far ahead of them, a RUSTLE…

And then there lumbered into view

    A lone gorilla, then a few.

Now that the guide at last had found them
These massive beasts were all around them!
Gorillas left, gorillas right,
Gorillas everywhere in sight!
And now, completely at their ease,
They started eating James's fleas,
While both his parents watched in awe,
Quite blown away by what they saw.

And while the apes had **fun and games**
Caressing, stressing, pressing James
(Who now was feeling less than sunny
And didn't find the whole thing funny)
His **odour** reached the chieftain's bed.
The Chief Gorilla stirred his head.

He took a sniff. He sniffed some more.

He'd smelt that scent somewhere before.

Methodically, he worked the snout

Then clambered up and squinted out …

(Another thing you ought to know:

That many, many years ago

Some hunters, armed with knives and guns,

Had snatched one of the chieftain's sons

And sold him to a far-off zoo,

Where, happily, he lived and grew.

Of course, the chieftain didn't know

His infant's circumstance, and so

He secretly had always yearned

That one day soon he'd be returned.)

The Chief Gorilla strained his eyes.

    This newcomer was small in size,

But then again, his SCENT was right!

    (Gorillas have no sense of sight

And so instead, they mostly tell

    Their kin apart by sense of smell.)

And now the chieftain was quite sure:

    He'd smelt this stranger's whiff before.

Could this outsider be the one?

    The Chief Gorilla's **LONG LOST SON**?

He bounded up, and with a frown

    He held the poor boy upside down

And peered at James, who now was quaking.

    Oh yes! There could be no mistaking.

And so what that this stranger's figure

    Might well have been a **trifle bigger**?

Who gave a damn his skin was fair?

So what that he was short on hair?
    They shouldn't mock his son's physique –
        He'd love this titchy, hairless freak!
And so he gave a **ROAR** of pride

        And clasped the young boy to his side,
Resolved to pamper and adore
        His infant son for evermore.

Now James's parents didn't see
        This roar was meant paternally,
And so they *yelped*, and altogether
        Turned tail and legged it hell for leather.
Poor James was done for. Total goner!
        Who gave a damn for love and honour?
If one thing signals 'stop exploring',
        It's surely a gorilla roaring.
And so – dumbfounded, dazed and damp –
        They staggered back into the camp,

Collapsed, and had a drink or two.

But still the question: what to do?

The guide was gone. They didn't dare

Go back to **find their son** and heir,

But goodness, how they felt regret!

James must be dead. He must. And yet …

It struck them that the Chief's complexion

Had carried something of affection.

Dad looked at Mum, beset by doubts.

He didn't know the ins and outs

But even so, a vague idea

Was growing steadily more clear.

'Er, darling – you know James's smell?

You don't think the gorillas, well …

Do you suppose they might have thought

That James was like them? Surely not …'

Mum turned away her tear-streaked face.

'You know, he's in a better place.
He'll never have to wash again.

He won't drive all his friends insane.
No more complaints from ANGRY teachers!

Yes, he's at home among those creatures.
D'you think that by Rwandan law,

We could, perhaps … well, say no more?'

They'd packed their bags the following day,

And, giving James's things away,
They soon enough were on a **plane**

And then, at long last, home again!
They left the whole affair at that.

He'd found his natural habitat,
And really, when they lost their son,

Well … everybody sort of won.
Today their house is fresh and clean,

Bereft of any **smelly teen**.
(*Er, Nell?* I hear you cry, but no:

Girls never sweat, they merely glow.)
The chieftain also came out well;

He loves James and his pleasing smell,
And nowadays the boy's revered

(Although the monkeys find him weird).

But as for James – he paid the price.

    He tried escaping once or twice,

And yet, his would-be great escapes

    Were swiftly thwarted by the apes

Who just assumed this fair-skinned freak

    Was keen on playing hide-and-seek.

The chieftain loved to watch them play,

    And so he **HUGGED** James every day

And clasped him tight and let him know

    He'd never, *ever* let him go.

And now, there's one last thing to say:

    When young Rwandan boys today

Refuse to wash and start to **smell**

    Their clever mothers often tell

A fearful story of a wild

    And rather SAVAGE monkey-child

Who snatches children from their beds

    Then eats them and collects their heads,

And yet, who'll never deign to eat

    A youngster who is clean and neat.

And who inspires these gruesome claims?

    Who else but pungent, putrid James!

You may think this a trifle gory,

    But there's a moral to the story:

If you don't want to be devoured,

    Well then, perhaps it's time you showered.

Mabel

Who texted so much that she forgot how to speak

The swiftest, surest teenage phase,

    Which seems pandemic nowadays,

Is that most adolescent crime

    Of texting *all the bloody time.*

I'm sure you know the famous case:

    A girl by name of Mabel Chase

Who disregarded all advice

    And – oh, poor child! – who paid the price.

A **classic** dinner-time routine

    Would see her family convene,

And sit around the dinner table.

    They'd talk – but wait! Not so with Mabel.

For while her family conversed,

    The girl would plunge herself head-first

Into the world of **CYBERSPACE**:

    Has Ashley got to second base?

Is Valentino really straight?

    Has Katy Perry lost some weight

Is Dylan going out with Joan?

    OMFG, I ♥ my phone.

Her parents cared not one amoeba
  About the trials of Justin Bieber,
And yet their daughter's greatest passion
  Stood **SQUARELY** in the latest fashion.
They ate their dinners, quite unable
  To get a single word from Mabel,
And though they talked of Bach or Proust,
  For her, the iPhone ruled the roost.

While texting, she avoided waffle,
  Expressing humour with a 'ROFL'.
Or, finding something very droll,
  She'd move to 'haha, luv it, LOL',
What else to say? She thought quite highly
  Of those who ended with a ☺,
She always gossiped with her sex
  Whenever boys signed off with x,
And oh! She found it just repelling
  When people used the proper spelling.

She lived in textspeak. I'll translate.

 If something's good, you say it's 'gr8'.
'IDK' means 'I don't know',

 While 'g2g' means 'got to go',
A ghastly fellow is a 'h8er',

 'Adieu' translates as 'c ya l8er',
'OMFG' means 'Well, I'm struck!'

 And 'F' is almost always 'F***'.

ROFL

ha ha ha LoL

g2g × ×

c ya l8ter x

OMFG (əʊemeʃˈdʒiː) *exclamation* [INFORMAL]

Used to express significant levels of excitement, surprise, disbelief ...etc.

 e.g. OMFG, this book is so awesome!

And so this stupid, smarmy kid
Would seldom talk – oh God forbid! –

 But roamed around, like any teen,
Her eyes glued to her iPhone screen,

 Quite disengaged and dumb and deaf
To all except her BFF.

 In lessons she was quite perplexed
When teachers told her not to text,

 And though she tried she couldn't see
The crime in saying 'OMG!'

 What brought about their discontent?
They knew exactly what she meant!

 Why *should* she use the proper word
Instead of one which she preferred?

Why couldn't adults be more lenient,
When textspeak was just so *convenient*?

It happened on some **summer's day**,
    Around the second week of May.
She was at school. Her phone was out.
    The girl was reading all about
Some party which had been arranged,
    When – **snap!** – the wind abruptly changed.
She didn't notice it at first,
    But when her teacher tripped and cursed
She softly murmured 'ROFLMAO'.

    Her teacher knitted up his brow
(For it was his especial foible
    To get cantankerous with Mabel).
'Excuse me, Chase, what *did* you say?'
    She paused, and answered, 'IDK.'
'Enough!' His chest began to swell.
    She only whispered, 'FML …'
'That's it! Too much!' he clamoured, rising.
    'Your constant lingual bastardising
Is over. I'll have Mrs Grey
    Ring up your parents straight away.'
She fled the room and dried her eyes.

Her parents came in much surprise,
And so it was that Mabel Chase
    Was driven homewards in disgrace.

'But *why?*' said Mum. 'For heaven's sake!
    Just talk! There must be some mistake.'
Poor Mabel, for the umpteenth time,
    Using the medium of mime
Attempted to communicate

    The reason for her speechless state
Her father, who was in the City,
    Said, 'Dearie me, this is a pity.
God bless my soul, whatever next?
    Mab, *can you talk?*'

`'Hmm-hmm, in txt.'`
    Then Dad, although a quiet fellow,
Went green and grey and red and yellow,
    Before he whooped and cried, '**EUREKA!**
She's textspeak's only fluent speaker.

Now call the doctor! Call the police!
I'll organise a press-release.
   Ring up the tabloids, get the *Sun* –
They'll die for this! They'll pay a ton.
   The headlines – I can see them now:
GIRL SPEAKS IN TEXT … Cor blimey! Wow!'

And now she's treated as a freak;
   She gets examined every week,
As surgeons try to find a cure –
   A fate no youngster should endure.
The papers too paid hefty fees
   To publicise this strange disease,
And though the fuss has since died down,
   Still Mabel feels like a clown.
Like Echo of the Greek myths, she
   Detests her vocal malady,
And now she only speaks in text.
   Who knows? Perhaps you might be next.

Tim

Who made sexist jokes and got exactly
what he was asking for

There was a boy whose name was Tim.

He really was extremely **dim**

And why was that? Well here's the gist:

He was a staunch misogynist.

For him, it seemed a near-religion

To mention women and 'the kitchen',

Or give a stupid, cocksure leer

And say, 'Hey babe – go fetch a beer.'

It made his sister **huff** and **puff**

Till one day she had had enough,

And so, the next time Timmy tried

To be all chauvinist and snide
She felt the need to interpose,
    And punched him squarely on the nose.
This gesture, pleasingly succinct,
    Made Timmy stop at once. He blinked,
Then oh, you should have heard him **bawl**!
    And frankly, he deserved it all.

Felicia

Who took forever in the shower and became permanently shrivelled

Felicia had it in her power
To spend whole mornings in the shower.
Alas, this was unwise – for soon,
Her nickname was The Human Prune.

Ted

Who was always hopelessly pretentious and starved as a result

Let's introduce you now to Ted –

Or, as he very often said,

Eduardo Quinn Delaney Hurd

Godolphin Chumley-Coombes the Third.

(You may well LAUGH, and rightly so.

It tells you all you need to know.)

Young Teddy, at the age of four,

Had called his father immature,

And thereby set the tone that would

Define and mould his life for good;

He'd never use a **word or two**

Where half a dozen more would do,

And always rambled in a chorus

Of phrases straight from his thesaurus.

The way he talked was rather great:

You don't spit, you expectorate;

A thing's not smart, it's perspicacious;

You're never greedy, you're voracious;

A silly deed is injudicious

Or maybe overly ambitious

Or needing one who's switched his brain on!

('Why isn't that a *sine qua non*?')

Of course, his airs were not confined
    To verbal tics of such a kind.
At only thirteen years of age
    He thought that tweed was all the rage,
And liked to smoke the odd **cigar**
    And almost lived off caviar.

(To cater for him could be tough –
    We'll get to that part soon enough …)
There's naturally much more than that.
    The **pompous**, peevish little brat
Was listless, silly, vain and choosy,
    And only listened to Debussy,
And thought himself a man of stature,
    And said he was a child of Thatcher,
And only drank DARJEELING tea,
    And even quoted poetry!

(And not the good stuff – Kipling, Tennyson,
    Long tales of war and roasted venison –
But soppy, sappy, gooey tripe,
    All soupy-rich and overripe,
Which talked of lovers in their prime
    And sometimes didn't even *rhyme*.)

And so you see: he was, in short,
    A pompous, *flowery-shirted* wart.

You've got the point, so let's change tack.
    In class, young Ted had fallen back,
In part because he liked to shirk
    From anything that looked like work.
His grades had soon dropped through the floor,
    Yet still he slacked off more and more,
Till at the very end of term,
    His school card made his parents squirm.
Mathematics: Ghastly. *Science*: Awful.
    Italian: Often prone to waffle.
Design: Not good. I've had to scold …
    PE: He couldn't catch a cold!

So though they doted on their boy,
    His parents weren't quite wild with joy,
And soon were pondering, as one,
    The question of what could be done.
Mum snivelled. Dad began to fuss.
    'Dear – Ted has disappointed us.
No more the land of milk and honey!
    We'll cut off all his pocket money,
And institute a brand-new rule

That he's to go to summer school.'
(A necessary chore, if cruel.)
    Well Ted was less than happy, true,
But there was nothing he could do!
    His mum and dad would not relent;
They'd said exactly what they'd meant!
    So **summer** came, and off he went.

These kinds of courses often vary.
    Some are great, and some are scary.
Some are dull, and some diverting,
    Some are only good for flirting,
But if they share a single trait,
    It's that the **FOOD** is seldom great.
They're not deliberately mean –
    They just can't manage haute cuisine,
And kids are generally okay
    To wolf down junk three times a day
(Though naturally it gets quite tricky
    With kids who are, by nature, picky).

Well, Ted was pretty pleased at first.
    Despite the way he'd been coerced,
He **settled down** and made some chums
    And spent the morning doing sums
And felt in quite a cheerful mood

When it, at last, was time for food.

  By gum, he had an **appetite**!

What would he start with? Something light?

  An oyster dish? A plate of clams?

A platter full of uncured hams?

  A lobster tail? Some ravioli?

Some scrumptious, sumptuous guacamole?

  Oh this would all be very fine!

Young Ted edged forwards in the line

  And pictured plates of escargots,

And soon was at the front … but oh!

The dinner lady looked quite **frumpy**,

  Disinterested and vaguely grumpy,

And – **eurgh**! – there could be no disguising:

  The food was less than appetising.

Ted felt a shudder of dismay.
Before his eyes, a STEAMING tray
Of brownish, broiling, bubbling meat
Was clearly meant for him to eat!

The dinner lady's face was grim.
Without a word, she glared at him,
And, going by his hair and clothes,
Adjudged him to be *one of those*.
Poor Teddy quailed. 'Er … pardon me –
But what's all this supposed to be?'
She **fixed him** with a beady eye.
The little twerp. 'It's shepherd's pie.'
Ted tried to gulp, without success.
He'd have to force it down – unless …
At once, a thought ran through his head.
A surge of courage came to Ted,
And so he piped up, feeling **macho**,
'I guess you don't do beef carpaccio?'
The answer came quite quickly. 'No.'
'Or maybe a *blanquette de veau*?'
'I'm sorry—' 'Or some cassoulet?'
'We—' 'Or perhaps a cheese soufflé?'
'You—' 'Or a nice sole *meunière*?
Or foie gras? Or some Camembert?

Or *coq au vin?* Or fresh-seared ling?
    Or really, frankly, *anything?*'

The lady, though quite short and stout,
    Shot Ted a killer **death-ray** pout
And told him straight: 'It's this or nowt.'

At times like this, you can't help feeling
    That though it might be unappealing
It's better to suppress your frown,
    And get the **ghastly** foodstuff down.
This line of thought occurred to Ted,
    Who very nearly vomited.
Oh no, no, no! He felt defeated.
    He couldn't bring himself to eat it!
Thirteen full years of **being picky**
    Had made his situation sticky,
For as the meat *frothed up* and spumed,
    The boy felt absolutely doomed.
Inside his head, the words rang out
    ('Mwah-ha-ha-ha. It's this or nowt.')
But if he ate – could they not see? –
    His next stop would be A&E!

A smallish whimper came from Ted,
Who dropped his plate and turned and fled
    And felt the colour leave his cheeks
And wouldn't eat for weeks and weeks.
    You need not be a dietician
To know this is an ●▮▮ position.
    In fact, Ted died of malnutrition.

Melissa

Who lost both her legs because she wore skinny jeans the entire time

Melissa Blagg, my sister's friend,

    Wore **skinny jeans** for days on end

And flaunted them at home and school

    And wore them to the swimming pool,

And even kept them on at night!

    Of course, the jeans were far too tight

And stopped the blood flow, sad to tell,

    Until her legs began TO SWELL.

This kind of thing is seldom great,

    And hers was an unhappy fate:

Alas, they had to amputate.

Sam

Whose inability to satisfy his evil teacher led to an untimely death

This poem was written in a single night in an attempt to placate my maths teacher, who had set a piece of homework that I could not even come close to understanding. His identity has of course been cunningly disguised. Fortunately, he had a sense of humour about the whole thing.

Young Samuel was a *charming* child
    Who loved to laugh and often smiled.
The boy would play for hours on end
    At cops and robbers with a friend,
Or they would re-enact, outdoors,
    The **full Napoleonic Wars**.
He lived a healthy life, and full
    Of candy, clothes and cotton wool,
But though you searched, you could not find
    A boy more grateful, warm, and kind.
Back then, he knew not of the strife
    Which soon would tear apart his life;
For scarcely had he turned fourteen,
    When – **ah!** – along came Mr Greene.

It's strange how many psychopaths
    Now earn a living teaching maths,
When they, by rights, should really be
    Deep in some penitentiary.
A viler man you never saw.
    It's doubtful whether British law
Permits such methods as he used
    To punish boys who looked confused.
He'd whip the poor, misguided fool
    Who didn't get the product rule,
And problems over integration
    Would warrant on-the-spot castration,
While pupils who could not derive
    Would seldom leave the room **alive**.
And yet, this vile, sadistic sham
    Took special joy tormenting Sam.
He'd see the poor boy's work, and then –
    'Of course not! **STUPID!** Try again!'

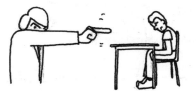

Young Sam would SWEAT and slave away
  On large expansions, day by day,
While Mr Greene grew more fanatical,
  Revering all things mathematical.

One day, the teacher slowly smiled.
  'Well, well, my children. I've compiled
A list of very simple sums.
  And as we all are such great chums
Perhaps you'd be so good to delve
  Right into questions 1 to 12.'
And of this work, the merest sight
  Sent Sam a-quivering with fright.

He closed the door, and turned the lock,
  And slipped into a state of shock.
They found him on the following day;
  The doc was summoned straight away,
And rushing to the infant's bed,

  He stopped, and looked, and shook his head.
'Gross overwork or something close is
  My professional diagnosis.

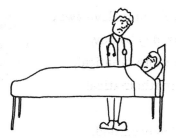

There is no **cure**; at best I'd give
 Young Sam about a day to live.'
And his prediction did not fail.
 What is the moral of this tale?
Avoid sadistic psychopaths
 By taking English over maths.

Acknowledgements

My acknowledgements are split four ways:

First, to Miranda Kazantzis, for being such an
unsparingly dutiful and loving godmother despite
a long-running absence of thank you letters;

Second, to all the teachers who have inspired,
encouraged and taken the mickey out of me – in
particular, Paul Smith, Charles Milne, and Simon
Dean, to whom I owe gratitude, subject matter
and overcoats;

Third, to James, René, Anna and Juj Leader, who have
taught these poems in multiple settings, and have
never once failed to be welcoming, witty, brilliant,
kind and generous;

And lastly, to my family. Thank you for your help,
your humour, your love, your energy and your foibles,
without which this book could never have got off
the ground.